GET YOUR TRUTH BACK

THE ROADMAP FOR TEARING DOWN STRONGHOLDS

Dr. I. David Byrd

Copyright © 2020 by Destination Destiny

Get Your Truth Back, The Roadmap to Tearing Down Strongholds/ Byrd, I. David

ebook ISBN: 978-1-7354376-1-3
Paperback ISBN: 978-1-7354376-0-6
Library of Congress Control Number: 2020913687

No portion of this book may be reproduced, scanned, or distributed in any form without the written permission of the Publisher. Please purchase only authorized editions. For more information, address:

Destination Destiny
333 W. North Ave, Suite 330
Chicago, IL 60610

Copyright, Legal Notice, and Disclaimer:
This publication is protected under the US Copyright Act of 1976 and all other applicable international, federal, state, and local laws, and all rights are reserved, including resale rights. If you purchase this book without a cover, you should be aware that this book is stolen property. I was reported as "unsold" or "destroyed" to the publisher, and neither the author nor the publisher has received any payment for this "stripped book."

Please note that much of this publication is based on personal experience and anecdotal evidence. Although the author and publisher have made every reasonable attempt to achieve complete accuracy of the content, they assume no responsibility for errors or omissions. Also, you should use this information as you see fit, and at your own risk. Your particular situation may not be exactly suited to the examples illustrated here; you should adjust your use of the information and recommendations accordingly. Meant to inform and entertain the reader, nothing in this book should replace common sense, legal, medical, or other professional advice.

Any trademarks, service marks, products names, or named features are assumed to be the property of their respective owners and are used only for reference. There is no implied endorsement if we use one of these terms.

Cover Design: Majestic Ink Design
Book Design: Word-2-Kindle, adapted for ebook

TABLE OF CONTENTS

Forward..1
Why You Need This eWorkbook 3
Instructions for Participating....................................5

The Provocative Approach

1 *The Stronghold Story*..9
2 **ESTIMATES** — *satan's strategies for your defeat and destruction* 14
3 **ENTREAT** *the Lord in Prayer as you embark on a Plan* 22

The Practical Plan

4 **ESTEEM IT** *(What Is)* 29
   Identify *the behavior patterns controlling your thoughts*

5 **EXPLAIN IT** *(Who's Affected)*...............................37
   Unpack *the origins of those thought patterns*

6 **EVALUATE IT** *(What Should Be)* 45
   Create *a vision of the future, free of the strongholds that hinder doing what God has called you to do*

7 **EFFECTUATE IT** *(Spiritual Gap)*............................51
   Surround *your strongholds with the Word of God*

8 **EXCHANGE IT** *(Gap Closure)* 61
   Design *the actions to take back your truth and authority*

9 **ENHANCE IT** *(Success Partner)* 74
   Prepare *your Take Back Your Truth Manifesto*

10 **EXECUTE IT** *(Spiritual Vitality)*............................ 84
   Implement *your battle plan*

11 **ELIMINATE IT** *(Flourishing)* 90
   Teardown *your strongholds*

EUPERISTATOS – The Conclusion........................ 93

Forward

Wherefore seeing we also are compassed about with so great a cloud of witnesses, let us lay aside every weight, and the sin which doth so easily beset us, and let us run with patience the race that is set before us.

Hebrew 12:1

Throughout Scripture, God used questions to enhance the change He was making in the lives of individuals. He wanted His listeners to think. It facilitates the learning process in each of us. In the Old Testament, He asked Adam, *"Why are you hiding?"* He asked Job, *"Where were you when I formed this world?"* In the New Testament, He asked the rich young ruler, *"What does the Scripture say?"* He asked His followers, *"Who do you say I am"*. Each module will provide a set of appropriately challenging, engaging, and compelling questions to help you unpack and address the root causes of your strongholds. Collectively, they will ask you the question Jesus asked the invalid laying by the pool of Bethesda: *"Do you want to get well?"*

When seeking to make life changes, we often fail to plan, which is a plan to fail. Prov 19:2 speaks of *"Desire without proper knowledge is not good."* Corporate America's planning process identifies the current state, the future state, identifies the gap, and creates a gap closure plan. A Contractor would say, if you build a house, first sit down and count the cost. In the military, they say, ready, aim, fire. But the Christian plans differently. The Bible says, *"we wrestle not against flesh and blood."* As we dig deeper into God's purpose relative to planning, we learn that in our spiritual battles, *"the house is built by first getting knowledge and understanding."* (Proverbs 24:3-4) Then we can design the change initiatives by *"writing the vision and make it plain.*" (Hab. 2:2)

If change were easy, perhaps more people would embrace it. However, if you research *Repetition Compulsion,* you will learn why so many people struggle to make change. Change opposes established neuropathways that compel us to repeat past behaviors. Upholding the status quo isn't just socially comfortable; it's biologically ingrained in the human mind. Our compulsive and self-oriented world has a firm grip on us, and we need a very strong and persistent discipline not to be squeezed to death by it. Let our false, compulsive self be transformed into the new self of Jesus Christ. It's the place where the old self dies and the new self is born, the place where the emergence of the new man and the new woman occurs.

This series sits at the intersection of theology, corporate methodology, and psychology. This series will put you on the path of holistic transformation of your mind, body, and soul to get your truth back. At the conclusion of working through this book, your uncontrolled carnal sin will be transformed to Jesus standards, whose completed victory is the enabling cause as well as the earnest of our own – *Euperistatos*. It's the Greek word meaning *well-positioned in every situation.*

Why You Need This eWorkbook

Shoddy thinking is costly to our witness
When Christians know God's will and do otherwise, the MIND is the access gate satan has used to get at your Spirit! We then accept as unchangeable situations that we know are contrary to the will of God. Excellence in thought, however, must be systematically cultivated.

This experience enhances your spiritual walk
Each chapter will provide a set of appropriately challenging, engaging, and compelling questions and exercises to help participants unpack and address the root causes of strongholds. Collectively, they will ask the question that Jesus asked the invalid laying by the pool of Bethesda, *"Do you want to get well?"*

A practical oriented methodology draws you into action
This Distributed Learning methodology sits at the intersection of theology, corporate methodology, and psychology. As a practical application, it means formulating answers to questions – not just reading or hearing. This type of learning encourages digging into memories for lessons already learned and helps create relevant connections and critical thinking skills to enhance support of your transformational objectives.

The intersections of Dr. Byrd's life work. Who God calls, He equips.
He is an ordained minister who brings his ministerial calling and corporate experiences into a union of service to the body of Christ. He serves as a preacher, teacher, author, mentor, coach, adjunct professor and workshop facilitator for those seeking to engage in critical conversations on the most

pressing issues facing individuals and the Church. His research, work and teaching have impacted lives across denominational, generational, and cultural boundaries. He focuses on the effects of cultural practices and norms on *identity development* in different social locations. Making the unconscious, conscious, his work unpacks how stereotypical life narratives (beliefs) will determine how you label someone. Labels, in turn, will influence the actions you engage in valuing or devaluing them—the antithesis of loving our neighbor.

He is a nondenominational servant with a Pentecostal upbringing. He has served at mega and small churches as Youth Pastor, Sunday School Teacher, Men's Ministry Facilitator, Prayer line, Business Engagement, and Baptismal team member. He possesses over 30 years of corporate leadership experience, converting strategy into effective execution for achieving operational excellence in the private & public sectors of Fortune 50 to small start-ups.

Educationally, He received his Dmin at McCormick Theological Seminary in Chicago. MBA from Carnegie Mellon Tepper School of Business in Pittsburgh and McCormick Theological Seminary in Chicago. His undergraduate degree in Computer Science and Business Management is from the University of Dayton in Dayton, Ohio. He sits on several Christian and secular Boards. He is married to his girlfriend and best friend, Monique.

Instructions For Participating

Before you start, gather the following materials:
- a pen or pencil;
- an extra notebook, just in case you want to take notes outside the document;
- Your Bible – 2 different translations will provide the best experience;

Plan to spend 15 minutes per day working through the activities; however we understand that each person is unique and this general estimate may vary for each individual.

Part 1, *The Provocative Approach*, provides an overview of how strongholds develop, an understanding of satan's ways of creating those strongholds in your life, and the role of prayer in connecting you to God's power to create a plan to **Get Your Truth Back.**

Part 2, *The Practical Plan* begins developing your action plan to identify and teardown your strongholds. The most effective way to benefit from this experience is to begin each chapter with a word of prayer and a few minutes of silence to settle your mind. Set the stresses and distractions of the day aside and lean into this process. You will be tempted to quickly answer the questions and think, *I'm done, Next.* But take your time; each chapter is designed for a week of reflection. If you are asked to talk to others about a subject, do it. Don't skip that step. This is an workbook and where ever you see the symbol 📖 space is provided to capture your thoughts as you progress through each question. You should read each scripture presented in two different translations. Why? Many of us spend more time reading or listening to someone else's take on Scripture than reading it. The revelation comes through personal conversations with the text. You will be amazed at how this will enhance your understanding of the Scripture. We have provided a separate page for additional notes or reflections at the end of each chapter.

The degree to which you embrace the process determines the level of transformation you will achieve.

THE PROVOCATIVE APPROACH

1. The Stronghold Story

THE TRUTH WILL SET YOU FREE

The Christian journey is full of potholes on the road to sanctification. As you grow in grace, you change your life by changing how you think and act. Jesus confirmed the connection between our hearts and our minds, which in turn affects our actions. *"We become what we think."* (Prov. 23:7) In Matthew 15:19, he said, *"For out of the heart come evil thoughts, murder, adultery, sexual immorality, theft, false testimony, slander."* Infidelity was a thought before it became an act. Theft started as an idea before it evolved into action. Your mind is the battleground for tearing down your strongholds. The earliest stage of the journey requires a clear understanding of where you are, and how you got there. Then you will appreciate the worthiness of the task at hand, and you can find value in the victory.

In one of his books, Frangipane wrote, "What men call "salvation" is simply the first stage of God's plan for our lives, which is to conform us in character and power to the image of Jesus Christ. If we fail to see our relationship to God as such, we will allow too many areas within us to remain unchanged. Pulling down strongholds is the demolition and removal of these old ways of thinking so that the actual Presence of Jesus Christ can be manifested through us."

Another Pastor speaks of strongholds as "A sin or a sinful attitude or habit that is fortified or strengthened by a worldview until you can't overcome it." A worldview is defined as a particular philosophy of life or concept(view) of the world held by an individual. It is the lens through which you see and filter everything in life. Further, he says, "If the worldview is Christian and Godly... your thinking, conscience, and actions will be. If the worldview is worldly, unchristian, materialistic... your thinking, conscience and actions will be". Ed Silvoso defines a stronghold as "a mindset impregnated with hopelessness that causes us to accept something that we know is contrary to the will of God." Either the sin or the worldview can be deeply entrenched and nearly impossible to demolish. A stronghold is a besetting sin that we on our own can't rid. A fortified area in our life, where satan has built a wall around a sin.

I've synthesized the words of several Pastors to answer the question of where do strongholds come from, how they are established, and what is their purpose?

Before we get saved, we are carnal and at enmity with God. We have a worldly, carnal, sinful nature. Our hearts and minds are polluted by sinful strongholds that satan has established in us. Footholds are territory that you surrender to satan. He cannot make you do anything. The enemy has no power to take your territory, your mind, or your heart. But he can squat on any territory you willingly surrender, and when you do, he gets a foothold, an opening, you surrender an area of your mind, territory, or life to him. When satan gets enough of these footholds in your territory, your nature, your worldview, your conscience become evil.

When we get saved, we get a new nature and a new mission. A mission to take possession of our territory and bring it under the rule and reign of God. The enemy, the former inhabitant of that territory which you surrendered, has no intention of being forced out without a fight. The enemy knows there is nothing he can do to snatch your soul from God's hand. He knows you are lost to him when you get saved. BUT

<u>**He knows that though he has lost your eternal soul, your flesh is still very much at his disposal.**</u>

So, those areas where you give him an inch allow you to open yourself to sin without any long-range thoughts. Those are the footholds the enemy will fortify. 1 Peter 5:8 tells us to, *"Be sober and watch: because your adversary the devil, as a roaring lion, goeth about seeking whom he may devour."* These footholds in the mind and flesh are all satan has left, and He knows the Holy Spirit is going to convict you to get rid of these footholds. As soon as satan gets a foothold in your life, he immediately sets about turning the FOOTHOLD into a STRONGHOLD.

Now let's apply Scripture to this problem to assist you in breaking the strongholds that distract you on the road to your DESTINY. The Apostle Paul in 2 Corinthians 10:5-6 defines strongholds as *"speculations or lofty things raised against the knowledge of God. "It is any type of thinking that exalts itself above the knowledge of God, thereby giving the devil a secure place of influence in an individual."* Additionally, Phil 2:5 says, *"Let this mind be in you, which was also in Christ Jesus."* The Scripture is speaking of breaking patterns of thinking and beliefs that are not of Him. God is saying to us; I don't want you to think about things the way you would think about them. I want you to think about them the way I think about them. In other words, *reject the world's way of thinking.* (Ephesians 4:17) When we humbly seek His guidance and are *"renewed in the spirit of our mind" (Eph. 4:23),* there is nothing we can't overcome, and we begin to live in His truth.

Your transformation, just like your faith, can awaken in an instant but blooms gradually. It's the seed that must first take root in your heart and mind, and then it grows to bear fruit. You're not reading this by accident. No matter where you are in your spiritual journey, it's time to declare and decree – I'm coming out of this. I'm ready to take back my truth!

Father, on our own, we can do nothing. But with you all things are possible. Your Word tells us that "if we keep our mind stayed on You, You will keep us in perfect peace." So today, we surrender our strongholds to You. Forgive us, cleanse our hearts, and renew our minds. We thank you for those you will put in our lives to walk alongside us as we work to break these strongholds. In Jesus' Name. Amen

NOTE: Adapted from Franco Frangipane, The Three Battle Grounds

2. ESTIMATES

Satan's strategies for your defeat and destruction

The prerequisite to victory is to make proper preparation. War is to be preceded by measures designed to win. Scripture teaches us that we will win if we follow the Biblical guidelines for winning spiritual battles. The warfare of satan is based on deception. His primary target is the mind. Let's take a moment to call out satan's mode or system of rule.

ESTIMATES – *SATAN'S STRATEGIES FOR YOUR DEFEAT AND DESTRUCTION*

> PRAYER
>
> Father God help me to see that the tricks of the enemy are not for my good. Prune every ungodly distraction that is not expedient for me. I am not ignorant to satan's devices and I understand his only plan is to rob me of the DESTINY You have for my life. Help me to see the spirit behind the temptations. In Jesus name I pray. Amen

Be well-balanced – temperate, sober minded; be vigilant and cautious at all times. For the enemy of your mind, the devil, roams around like a lion roaring in fierce hunger, seeking someone to seize upon and devour.

Satan's General Strategy

1. *"Stand against the wiles of the devil" (Ephesians 6:11)*
    A settled plan, to plan crafty tricks and schemes

2. *". . . in order that satan might not take advantage" (2 Corinthians 2:11)*
    Wanting more, to take the greater part, to plunder

3. *". . . for we are not unaware of his schemes" (2 Corinthians 2:11)*
    To plan very meticulously, to strategize

Satan's Specific Strategy

1. **Quickly snatching away the spiritual seeds sown into our hearts through preaching, prayer and testimony before the seed can take root**

   Matthew 13:19 - When anyone hears the message about the kingdom and does not understand it, the evil one comes and snatches away what was sown in their heart. This is the seed sown along the path.

2. **Quietly and persistently take away your spiritual rights and the spiritual ground God has given you, setting up his ownership little by little.**

   Ephesians 4:1 - As a prisoner for the Lord, then, I urge you to live a life worthy of the calling you have received.

3. **Repeatedly using the art of condemnation to shake our assurance, cripple our confidence, and devastate our future hopes and dreams**

   Revelations 12:9-11 - The great dragon was hurled down—that ancient serpent called the devil, or Satan, who leads the whole world astray. He was hurled to the earth, and his angels with him. Then I heard a loud voice in heaven say: "Now have come the salvation and the power and the kingdom of our God, and the authority of his Messiah. For the accuser of our brothers and sisters, who accuses them before our God day and night, has been hurled down. They triumphed over him by the blood of the Lamb and by the word of their testimony they did not love their lives so much as to shrink from death.

4. **Overwhelming our soul by a chain of unusual bad experiences, irritations, or small calamities so that he may destroy our faith and gain control over us through fear.**

   Matthew 17:15 - *"Lord, have mercy on my son," he said. "He has seizures and is suffering greatly. He often falls into the fire or into the water.*

   Acts 10:38 - *how God anointed Jesus of Nazareth with the Holy Spirit and power, and how he went around doing good and healing all who were under the power of the devil, because God was with him.*

   2 Corinthians 12:7 - *or because of these surpassingly great revelations. Therefore, in order to keep me from becoming conceited, I was given a thorn in my flesh, a messenger of Satan, to torment me.*

   Isaiah 59:19 - *From the west, people will fear the name of the Lord, and from the rising of the sun, they will revere his glory. For he will come like a pent-up flood that the breath of the Lord drives along.*

5. **Hindering the Church from moving into spiritual blessings by attacking key leaders or key people, creating a spirit of negativism, magnifying little problems, relational conflicts, producing spiritual unrest, murmuring; and anything that will cause division**

   2 Corinthians 6:1 - *We put no stumbling block in anyone's path, so that our ministry will not be discredited.*

Matthew 5:9 - *Blessed are the peacemakers, for they will be called children of God.*

Matthew 18:15 - *If your brother or sister sins, go and point out their fault, just between the two of you. If they listen to you, you have won them over.*

Ephesians 4:29 - *Do not let any unwholesome talk come out of your mouths, but only what is helpful for building others up according to their needs, that it may benefit those who listen.*

Hebrews 12:15 - *See to it that no one falls short of the grace of God and that no bitter root grows up to cause trouble and defile many.*

James 1:19-20 - *My dear brothers and sisters, take note of this: Everyone should be quick to listen, slow to speak and slow to become angry, because human anger does not produce the righteousness that God desires.*

Ecclesiastes 7:9 - *Do not be quickly provoked in your spirit, for anger resides in the lap of fools.*

Satan's Seasonal Strategy

While the attacks may not be continuous, they are strategic:

1. **Attacks in seasons of fruitfulness. To attack when you are unprepared.**

Genesis 49:22-26 - *"Joseph is a fruitful vine, a fruitful vine near a spring, whose branches climb over a wall. With bitterness archers attacked him; they shot at him with hostility. But his bow remained steady, his strong arms stayed limber, because of the hand of the Mighty One of Jacob, because of the Shepherd, the Rock of Israel, because of your father's God, who helps you, because of the Almighty, who blesses you with blessings of the skies above, blessings of the deep springs below, blessings of the breast and womb. Your father's blessings are greater than the blessings of the ancient mountains, than[d] the bounty of the age-old hills. Let all these rest on the head of Joseph, on the brow of the prince among his brothers.*

2. **Attacks in seasons of sacrifice. To keep you under strain and wear you down.**

   Genesis 15:11 *- Then birds of prey came down on the carcasses, but Abram drove them away.*

   Matthew 18:18-23 - *"Truly I tell you, whatever you bind on earth will be bound in heaven, and whatever you loose on earth will be loosed in heaven. "Again, truly I tell you that if two of you on earth agree about anything they ask for, it will be done for them by my Father in heaven. For where two or three gather in my name, there am I with them." Then Peter came to Jesus and asked, "Lord, how many times shall I forgive my brother or sister who sins against me? Up to seven times?" Jesus answered, "I tell you, not seven times, but seventy-seven times. "Therefore, the kingdom of heaven is like a king who wanted to settle accounts with his servants.*

3. **Attacks in seasons of breakthrough. To divide when you are united.**

    Exodus 14:15-16 - *Then the Lord said to Moses, "Why are you crying out to me? Tell the Israelites to move on. Raise your staff and stretch out your hand over the sea to divide the water so that the Israelites can go through the sea on dry ground.*

    1 Corinthians 16:9 - *Because a great door for effective work has opened to me, and there are many who oppose me.*

4. **Attacks in seasons of intense prayer intercession. To create disorder that distracts you.**

    Daniel 9:3-4 - *So I turned to the Lord God and pleaded with him in prayer and petition, in fasting, and in sackcloth and ashes. I prayed to the Lord my God and confessed: "Lord, the great and awesome God, who keeps his covenant of love with those who love him and keep his commandments,*

    Daniel 10:12-14 - *Then he continued, "Do not be afraid, Daniel. Since the first day that you set your mind to gain understanding and to humble yourself before your God, your words were heard, and I have come in response to them.* **13** *But the prince of the Persian kingdom resisted me twenty-one days. Then Michael, one of the chief princes, came to help me, because I was detained there with the king of Persia. Now I have come to explain to you what will happen to your people in the future, for the vision concerns a time yet to come."*

Now you know his war plan to destroy you. Plan accordingly to take back your truth.

NOTE: Adapted from *Lay Pastor Training Manual*, Frank Damazio

3. ENTREAT

The Lord In Prayer As You Work On Your plan

Effective prayer is not about a one-way conversation with God. But taking time to hear God in conversation. Prayer at times requires waiting to hear God's answer. Going deep to allow our hearts to connect with God. That He may remake us daily. We must find ways to remove the distractions that can interrupt our time with God.

In our mind-oriented world, we will need a serious discipline to come to a prayer of the heart in which we can listen to the guidance of Him who prays in us. The emphasis of prayer is to help us discern which of our daily activities are indeed for the glory of God and which are primarily for the glory of our unconverted ego. There is an intimate relationship between prayer and your planning to tear down the strongholds in your life. As long as your focus is only about your problems, or about an endless number of activities which can hardly be coordinated; we are still very much dependent on our own narrow and anxious heart. But when our worries are led to the heart of God and there becomes prayer, then the prayers of the heart are the breath of the spiritual life.

Through prayer we can carry in our hearts all human pain and sorrow, all conflicts and agonies, all tortures and war, all hunger, loneliness, and misery, not because of some great psychological or emotional capacity, but because God's heart has become one with ours.

> *10 Finally, my brethren, be strong in the Lord and in the power of His might. 11 Put on the whole armor of God, that you may be able to stand against the wiles of the devil. 12 For we do not wrestle against flesh and blood, but against principalities, against powers, against the rulers of the darkness of this age, against spiritual hosts of wickedness in the heavenly places. 13 Therefore take up the whole armor of God, that you may be able to withstand in the evil day, and having done all, to stand.*
>
> *14 Stand therefore, having girded your waist with truth, having put on the breastplate of righteousness, 15 and having shod your feet with the preparation of the gospel of peace; 16 above all, taking the shield of faith with which you will be able to quench all the*

fiery darts of the wicked one. ***17*** *And take the helmet of salvation, and the sword of the Spirit, which is the word of God;* ***18*** *praying always with all prayer and supplication in the Spirit, being watchful to this end with all perseverance and supplication for all the saints—* ***19*** *and for me, that utterance may be given to me, that I may open my mouth boldly to make known the mystery of the gospel,* ***20*** *for which I am an ambassador in chains; that in it I may speak boldly, as I ought to speak.*

Ephesians 6:10-20

The powers and principalities not only reveal their presence in the unsettling political, economic, and personal situations of our day. They also show their disruptive presence in the most intimate places of our lives. Our faithfulness in relationships is severely tested, and our inner sense of belonging is questioned again and again. Our anger and greed show their strength with added vehemence, and our desire to indulge ourselves in the despairing hedonism of the moment proves to be stronger than ever. Our compulsive, wordy, and mind-oriented world has a firm grip on us and we need a very strong and persistent discipline not to be squeezed to death by it.[1]

---

[1] Adapted from *The Way Of The Heart*, Henri J. M. Nouwen, 1981

If God gives us orders to transform our lives, we can legitimately expect that He will also give us the tools we need to accomplish His purpose in our lives. **Getting Your Truth Back - *Tearing Down Strongholds*** *is one of those tools.*

Take a moment to list the "things" that you feel could distract you from spending time with God and beginning to create your plan for tearing down the strongholds that currently are controlling your attitudes and actions.	📖 this is my story

THE PRACTICAL PLAN

4. ESTEEM IT (What Is)

Identify the behavior patterns controlling your thoughts

Respect all strongholds because of the power they can have over your life. Esteeming means I take them seriously and realize they are a formidable opponent. To tear them down will require you to identify or name them. To identify a stronghold, you have to see it, so you know that with which you're dealing. But strongholds of the mind can be hidden and hang out in the darkness.

ESTEEM IT - *Ephesians 4:27*

> **PRAYER**
>
> All knowing God, I thank you for the desire to change my mindset. Help me to be honest with myself in this process. Keep my mind focused on thoughts that will edify the body of Christ. When the enemy tries to distract me, refocus my mind. In Jesus name we pray. Amen

Do you believe you have strongholds that you might not be aware of? *Explain*	

If you want to let the light of God expose your darkness, you need an attitude of humility and a willingness to let the light of God reveal your darkness.

In Psalms 26:2, David prayed, *"Test me, O LORD, and try me, examine my heart and my mind."* Pray this prayer and then jot down how this scriptural reference resonates with your thoughts at this point.	

- ✓ **Ephesians 5:11 urges us to** *"have nothing to do with the fruitless deeds of darkness, but rather expose them."* **Review the sinful patterns below and check those with which you struggle.**

❑ SELFISH AND SELF-SEEKING	❑ DISHONESTY	❑ FRIGHTENED	❑ INCONSIDERATE
❑ SELF JUSTIFICATION	❑ GREEDY	❑ LUSTFUL	❑ ANGER
❑ SELF IMPORTANCE	❑ SLOTH	❑ GLUTTONY	❑ IMPATIENT
❑ SELF CONDEMNATION	❑ PRIDEFUL	❑ ENVY	❑ SELF PITY
❑ HARMFUL ACTS	❑ SUSPICION	❑ DOUBT	❑ HATRED
❑ INTOLERANCE	❑ RESENTMENT	❑ APATHY	❑ REVENGE
❑ BLAME SHIFTER	❑ DECEPTION	❑ DEMANDING	❑ ABUSIVE
❑ DEFENSIVE	❑ CONTROLING	❑ RELIGIOSITY	❑ _____

- ✓ **Make copies of the next page**

- ✓ **Use the next page to ask <u>two</u> friends to select and prioritize the sinful patterns <u>they</u> feel are your struggle. Ask them why they prioritized them the way they did. Don't get into a back and forth with the person trying to defend yourself. There will be time for that in the future. Be open to honestly hearing what they tell you.** *Often others can see our patterns better than we can.*

- ✓ **Take notes on the conversation.**

BECAUSE YOU KNOW ME

I am embarking on a process to identify the sinful patterns in my life. Because you know me, I am asking you to assist me by doing 3 things:

1. **Selecting from the list below, what do you think are my sinful patterns. If what you think is not on this list, feel free to add it.**

   - ❏ SELFISH AND SELF-SEEKING
   - ❏ SELF JUSTIFICATION
   - ❏ SELF IMPORTANCE
   - ❏ SELF CONDEMNATION
   - ❏ HARMFUL ACTS
   - ❏ INTOLERANCE
   - ❏ BLAME SHIFTER
   - ❏ DEFENSIVE
   - ❏ DISHONESTY
   - ❏ GREEDY
   - ❏ SLOTH
   - ❏ PRIDEFUL
   - ❏ SUSPICION
   - ❏ RESENTMENT
   - ❏ DECEPTION
   - ❏ CONTROLING
   - ❏ FRIGHTENED
   - ❏ LUSTFUL
   - ❏ GLUTTONY
   - ❏ ENVY
   - ❏ DOUBT
   - ❏ APATHY
   - ❏ DEMANDING
   - ❏ RELIGIOSITY
   - ❏ INCONSIDERATE
   - ❏ ANGER
   - ❏ IMPATIENT
   - ❏ SELF PITY
   - ❏ HATRED
   - ❏ REVENGE
   - ❏ ABUSIVE
   - ❏ _____

2. **Can you go back and order those you have selected?**

3. **Give me examples of at least the first three (3) you choose. This will be beneficial for my understanding from someone else's perspective.**

Thank you for taking time to assist me in evaluating my patterns of behavior.

- ✓ **Compare and contrast the patterns on ALL three (3) lists.**

- ✓ **Using your notes from the discussions with friends, their prioritizations, and your prioritized list; create a list of your competing patterns in order of their destructive perspectives and behaviors on your life.**

- ✓ **Print 5 copies of the** Strongholds Worksheet – Part A **(see page 35)**

- ✓ **Utilize the** Strongholds Worksheets - Part A **(see page 35), list one of the sinful patterns of behavior on each of the five worksheets in Column 1 (Patterns).**

Example:

Pattern	How Manifested	Footholds
Column 1	Column 2	Column 3
Self-importance		

What was your rationale for choosing your number one sinful pattern?	

The mind is the citadel of the soul. He who controls the mind controls a very strategic place. But our conscious mind is not the target. Read Romans 8:5-6 and write your interpretations of what it is saying to you at this time.

- ✓ **Add to your Stronghold Worksheet – Part A in column 2 (How Manifested) how you feel each of the five sinful patterns manifest themselves in your life.**

Example: Stronghold Worksheet – Part A

Pattern	How Manifested	Footholds
Column 1	Column 2	Column 3
Self-importance	I tend to think I have all the answers.	

We are bringing your problems into the open. God lives in the land of light and honesty, and satan indwells the domain of shadows and secrets. God knows all about sinful patterns, and He knows how to take them. He'll tell you how to do it if you're willing to be honest and fight!

- ✓ **Review your worksheet over the balance of this week. If any additional thoughts on how those patterns manifest come to mind, that's okay. Just add them to column 2.**

If you want the abundant life and the peace that Jesus promised, you must let his Spirit capture the sinful patterns in your mind. Next week we will begin to **EXPLAIN IT**.

STRONGHOLD WORKSHEET – Part A

Patterns	How Manifested	Strongholds
Column 1	Column 2	Column 3
		Factors
		Environment
		Emotions
		Experienced or Secondhand Knowledge

NOTES

Throughout this module, capture your notes, reflections, and ideas in the space below. Make multiple copies if you need them.

Notes, Reflections, and Ideas

5. EXPLAIN IT (Who's Affected)

Unpack the origins of those thought patterns

Last week you discovered how your sinful patterns of behavior manifest themselves. This week you must find the origins of the footholds that have led to your strongholds. You will come to understand the actual effects and sources of the footholds controlling your thinking. "To thy own self be true."

EXPLAIN IT – *1 John 1:7*

> **PRAYER**
>
> Father, my list of destructive patterns are many. I bring them to you. Forgive me for allowing them to take up residence in my life. I seek to correct and change them, but I can only do it with your help. In Jesus' name. Amen

- ✓ **Start this week by reviewing your Stronghold Worksheet – PART A**

Once you recognize the patterns, the next step to bringing it down is repentance. Be honest before God, and humbly let the Spirit expose the footholds that are living in the darkness.

Now let's dig deeper to identify the footholds.

- ✓ **For each pattern, work through the following four questions. Use your note sheet if more space is needed.**

What factors from my past contribute to it?	

What in my environment is feeding it?	

What role are my emotions playing in it?	

Did the foothold come from my experience or secondhand knowledge? Explain	

✓ **Transfer your answers from above to column 3 (Footholds) of the Strongholds Worksheet Part A.**

Example: Stronghold Worksheet-Part A

Pattern	How Manifested	Footholds
Column 1	Column 2	Column 3
Self-importance	*I tend to think I have all the answers*	Teachers told me I was the best
		Others think too slow
		My achievements are exceptional

✓ **Lay each of the 5 Stronghold Worksheets side by side and review what you have entered in column 3. Use different color markers to highlight common footholds across all five pages.**

- ✓ **On Strongholds Worksheet Part B (page 43), pick one color, rewrite all that are that color in column 1 (Common Footholds). Repeat for each color. Draw a horizontal line to separate the different color groups.**

- ✓ **In column 2 (Thought Patterns), summarize, in one sentence, the critical thought pattern associated with each of these groupings of common footholds.**

Example: Stronghold Worksheet – Part B (page 43)

Common Footholds Column 1	Thought Patterns Column 2	Footholds Column 3
Others think too slow	I think I am better than others.	
My achievements are exceptional		

Those sinful patterns, a result of satan gaining footholds in your life, are the symptoms of a stronghold.

- ✓ **Look up in the dictionary or Google your patterns. Make notes as to what it says.**

Let's put it all together by translating your learnings about each pattern and footholds.

- ✓ **Name each grouping in column 3 (Strongholds) of Strongholds Worksheet Part B (page 43).**

Example: Stronghold Worksheet – *Part B*

Common Footholds	Thought Patterns	Footholds
Column 1	Column 2	Column 3
Others think too slow	I think I am better than others.	Haughty
My achievements are exceptional		

We all have multiple strongholds that need to be addressed. Based on reviewing columns 1 & 2, identify the top Stronghold in column 3 that most need your attention.

- ✓ **List the stronghold you selected**

    ✓ _____

We can now focus on the root causes of two negative thoughts that are controlling your mind. Yes, now we have your most controlling strongholds and are ready to do battle.

How are you feeling at this point?	

The poorest of all people is not the one without a nickel to his name. He is the fellow with a 10 x 12 capacity and a 2 x 4 soul.

Are you willing to do the work to break the stronghold you just identified? Why	

At this point, you may need to overcome the instinct to say I can't really overcome this. Don't worry, it's natural. You have to be willing to take every pattern of negative thinking captive and bring it to the obedience of God.

Read Proverbs 23:7 What is the importance of this verse at this point?	

- ✓ **Remember to bring Strongholds Worksheets-Parts A & B to next week's session.**

Next week we will **EVALUATE** your stronghold and paint a picture of victory. As Christians, we have the victory on the other side of glory. Our goal is the victory on this side of eternity.

STRONGHOLD WORKSHEET – Part B

Common Footholds	Thought Patterns	Strongholds
Column 1	Column 2	Column 3

NOTES

Throughout this module, capture your notes, reflections, and ideas in the space below. Feel free to make multiple copies if you need them.

Notes, Reflections, and Ideas

6. EVALUATE IT (What Should Be)

Create a vision of the future, free of the strongholds that hinder doing what God has called you to do

Last week we finished unpacking the footholds satan has used to create the strongholds in your life. You then selected the two most destructive strongholds to bring into this week. After this week, you will be able to visualize your life without the constraints that keep you from being all God has called you to be and to do. This view will strengthen you as you prepare to face the most challenging steps of moving from your current condition to what God intended you to be.

EVALUATE IT – *2 Corinthians 10:5*

> PRAYER
>
> Father, operating out of your will has affected so many people in my life. I desire to reconcile with them, but I know I must first come to the knowledge of how my thinking allowed me to get off course. Help me to be real with myself. In Jesus' name. Amen

✓ **Review** Stronghold Worksheet - B **from last week. Pay particular attention to the thought patterns you identified for each stronghold.**

It is important to note that when a stronghold is present in the life of a person, that spirit will influence the person to do what the spirit is there to do.

For example, a lying spirit makes a person tell lies; a lustful spirit makes people lust after particular things.

✓ **What spirits were you chasing that led to your strongholds?**

- ❏ THE AMERICAN DREAM
- ❏ CULTURE OF CHRIST
- ❏ A SPIRIT OF FEAR
- ❏ ECONOMIC ISSUES
- ❏ WRONG PERSPECTIVE
- ❏ KNOWLEDGE OF YOUR PURPOSE
- ❏ FAMILY ISSUES
- ❏ A FAULTY FOCUS
- ❏ A LACK OF TRUST
- ❏ COMPATATIVE NATURE
- ❏ OTHER _____

Which needs do you feel were not met that led to your stronghold? Circle all that apply	❏ Provision ❏ Protection ❏ Identity ❏ Comfort ❏ Teaching ❏ Companionship ❏ Communication ❏ Other _____

Who else is affected by your actions associated with your stronghold? List Names	

Describe, in detail, what they are experiencing, hearing, or seeing from you.	

What is this stronghold keeping you from doing for or with them?	

When thinking about your Strongholds, what are the false concepts that you believe to be true, but in reality, are not accurate?	
Describe life without this stronghold actively controlling your thinking.	
What positive things were gaining momentum in your life that this stronghold has derailed?	
What will be the benefits of breaking this stronghold?	

Every journey toward breaking a stronghold is personal, and as a result, so is the price that must be paid for it.

(Examples: Time commitment, uncomfortable conversations, letting a person go, submitting to authority, etc.)

Have you counted the cost? Are you willing to pay the price to break that stronghold?	

What do you think will be your biggest challenge to breaking this stronghold? *Remember, the dream is free, but the journey isn't!*	

Read Ephesians 2:6 and Colossians 3:1-2 How do these scriptures help you follow through until even the "ruins" of these strongholds are removed from your minds?	

Now you fully understand your stronghold, the effect on those around you, and what will be different when you have torn them down. You are ready for next week, where you will **EFFECTUATE** how the Word of God undergirds your planning.

NOTES

Throughout this module, capture your notes, reflections, and ideas in the space below. Feel free to make multiple copies if you need them.

Notes, Reflections, and Ideas

7. EFFECTUATE IT (Spiritual Gap)

Surround your strongholds with the Word of God

Last week we ultimately painted a picture of what your life would be like for you and those loved ones in your life when you take your truth back. This week we will learn how to implement God's Word, the only thing that will defeat a stronghold, to bring that future state picture into reality. This is not just about reading the Bible; **it's putting in the work** *from the Bible necessary to build your Spiritual muscles for the battle.*

EFFECTUATE IT – *John 17:15 - 17*

> **PRAYER**
>
> Father, your Word is the lamp that lights my path. Teach me your ways that I may see that I can change my thinking. In Jesus' name. Amen

Read Ephesians 4:1-32	
How does your calling set the stage for tearing down your strongholds? Take a moment to summarize in your notes how we should **think**, **talk,** and **treat** others.	

As followers of Christ, we must be committed to the truth. Our words should be honest, and our actions should reflect Christ's integrity.

How have your words and actions associated with your stronghold not lived up to these truths?	

Strongholds are the results of the lies the enemy has convinced you to believe are true. Let's review the Scriptures that undergird us.

In Spiritual warfare your weapon is using God's Word for defeating the enemy.

"You are of God, little children, and have overcome them, because He who is in you is greater than he who is in the world" (John 4:4)

"Yet in all these things we are more than conquerors through Him who loved us" (Romans 8:37)

"For though we walk in the flesh, we do not war according to the flesh. For the weapons of our warfare are not carnal but mighty in God for the pulling down strongholds (2 Corinthians 10:3-4)

"No weapon formed against you shall prosper, and every tongue which rises against you in judgement you shall condemn. This is the heritage of the servants of the Lord, and their righteousness is from me, say the LORD" (Isaiah 54:1)

"Yet Michael the archangel, in contending with the devil, when he disputed about the body of Moses, dared not bring against him a reviling accusation, but said, The Lord rebuke you! (Jude 1:9)

"The Lord will cause your enemies who rise against you to be defeated before your face; they shall come out against you one way and flee before you seven ways" (Deuteronomy 28:7)

"The angel of the Lord encamps all around those who fear Him, and delivers them" (Psalms 34:7)

"And they overcame him by the blood of the Lamb and by the word of their testimony, and they did not love their lives to the death". (Revelations 12:11)

"Therefore, submit to God. Resist the devil and he will flee from you. Draw near to God and He will draw near to you. Cleanse your hands, you sinners; and purify your hearts, you doubleminded" (James 4:7-8)

Now that you are undergirded by your war Scriptures, it's time to make your petitions known and see your problems from God's perspective.

- ✓ **Read each of the following Scriptures (from both translations you are using)**

Matthew 7:7-9

Matthew 18;19

Matthew 21:22

Luke 11:9-13

John 15:7

Ephesians 3:20

John 5:14-15

In summary, what do the scriptures above tell you?	

Read Gal 5:13	
What is the value of exercising self-control?	

Read Galatians 5:16-25	
Describe how you are conditioned to live oneway but are being pulled to live another?	

How will you use your mind to control your flesh?	

Now we are going to surround your stronghold's affirming the truth of God's Word.

✓ **Go to the Scripture to study the opposite truth from God.**
- *Ex: If your stronghold is rejection, study all that the Bible says about God's acceptance.*
- *Ex: If your stronghold is unresolved anger, study forgiveness*

Use a Concordance, a Chain Bible, or a Topical Bible to surround that stronghold with the Word of God!

Stronghold 1 _____	
What does the Bible say about it?	

Once the enemy is surrounded by humble submission, and the Word of God, his resistance will quickly weaken.

We can learn what faithfulness looks like under different circumstances from those in Scripture. Those similar to us and from those different than us.

✓ **Hebrews 12:1 tells us to study the Heroes of Faith, who have already dealt with our condition.**

Is there a Biblical character that had the same stronghold as you?	

✓ **Again, use a Concordance, a Chain Bible, or a Topical Bible.**

How did that character break their stronghold?	

Is additional research necessary to better understand this stronghold?	

Where can you find others with the same issue?	

Who can you talk to for a different perspective on the stronghold?	

✓ **Pick a few of the people you listed above to engage in conversation about your strongholds this week. Take notes about your discussions on your note sheet**

What did you learn from those conversations?	

You can get your truth back and live the life for which God created you, only after you figure it out. Why do you think you are ready?	

Are you willing to significantly change your priorities and habits to put into action what is needed? Why?	

There is an ancient story about the baby elephant being trained. A rope is put on its leg and then tied to a wooden post. The baby elephant, which is not very strong is unable to break it or pull up the post. Eventually it gives up. From this point forward, when the elephant's leg is secured, it *believes* it cannot get away - even when it is fully capable of escaping. It remembers its struggle. That's one reason it's said, "Elephants never forget."

- ✓ **Our thinking limits us, just like the elephant's does. If you give in to the thoughts and beliefs the enemy has convinced you are right, then you'll be right.**

The good news: fear of failure is common to all of us, yet we can overcome it. Know that, If God be for you, who can be against you.

- ✓ **Write an agreement to yourself that you can refer to when the going gets tough.**

	My Personal Commitment Statement
I believe God wants to do big things and He wants to do them through **you**. A desire confessed creates conflict; actions begin to create crisis. If you are ready to break your restraints. Declare and decree right now that you are ready.	

Next week we begin to **EXCHANGE** our old man and put on the new man that can stand up to the mental challenges of the enemy.

NOTES

Throughout this module, capture your notes, reflections, and ideas in the space below. Feel free to make multiple copies if you need them.

Notes, Reflections, and Ideas

8. EXCHANGE IT (Gap Closure)

Design the actions to take back your truth and authority

Last week we went to the Word to understand how we are spiritually equipped for pulling down our strongholds. This week we will make sure your thought process is in check. You have to use the right weapons for warfare and know how to use them properly. You will leave this week with a set of Strategic Initiatives designed to pull down the strongholds controlling your mind.

EXCHANGE IT – *Philippians 4:8-9*

> **PRAYER**
>
> Lord, to you, I turn over my mind and my thoughts. Inspire me to develop change initiatives that will take me to a new level of relationship with you. In Jesus' name. Amen

You now are ready to drop your ungodly strongholds and build up that one stronghold within your mind and heart – **the stronghold of the living God!**

Read 1 Thessalonians 5:5-11	
What are your weapons of warfare?	

What does it mean, to you, that the enemy no longer has authorized rule over your life? You authorized him, you gave it to him.	

What do you need to begin doing? (James 1:22)	

You can't dislodge him unless you dislodge him *legally* because you've given him a place.

✓ **Be done with it, confess it, forsake it. There's no other way to deal with sin.**

Make your confession to God.	

Even after you repent, the devil is not going to walk out. After repentance, there must be resistance.

"Resist the devil and he will flee from you." (James 4:7) What you gave him, take back. But you can never take it back until you take away the authority you gave him.

How successful have you been in the past resisting temptations?	

What was your strength in this time of weakness?	

✓ **Tell the devil:**

"I bring Jesus Christ against you. You have no right; you have no authority. This body of mine is the temple of the Holy Spirit of God. You are trespassing on my Father's property, and in the name of Jesus, whose I am and whom I serve, **it's time to go**.*"*

"And be renewed in the spirit of your mind; And that ye put on the new man, which after God is created in righteousness and true holiness" (Ephesians 4:23)

Why is it not enough to put off the old person but you must put on the new person?	

- ✓ **Take time and pray for guidance as you get ready to select the three actions to bring about your transition. We know our weapons are from God.**

You can't walk the second mile until you walk the first. You take the first actions and God will do the rest.

- ✓ **Use the next pages to write out the three drastic and specific actions to bring about your transition?**

Ex: If drinking is your stronghold; give Success Partner permission to smack you if you drink

When you write things down, you begin the process of activating the fundamentals in your life.

ACTION 1	**What can you start doing today to get closer to this action?**
Write the first Action	
	What can you do next to keep things moving?
	What will you need to do to consider this action complete?
BY WHEN	
When will it be done?	

WHAT MAKES THIS IMPORTANT?

HOW CAN YOU MEASURE SUCCESS FOR THIS ACTION?

ACTION 2 Write the first Action	**What can you start doing today to get closer to this action?**
	What can you do next to keep things moving?
	What will you need to do to consider this action complete?
BY WHEN When will it be done?	

WHAT MAKES THIS IMPORTANT?

HOW CAN YOU MEASURE SUCCESS FOR THIS ACTION?

ACTION 3	What can you start doing today to get closer to this action?
Write the first Action	
	What can you do next to keep things moving?
	What will you need to do to consider this action complete?
BY WHEN	
When will it be done?	

WHAT MAKES THIS IMPORTANT?

HOW CAN YOU MEASURE SUCCESS FOR THIS ACTION?

- ✓ **Do these actions seem radical? If not, you may need to rethink the three actions.**

Consecrate them and turn them over to the Lord	

After we have prayed and planned, planned and prayed, you must get up off your knees and prepare to take action!

Be careful of the thoughts you reflect on (Prov. 23:7). We cannot stop thoughts from entering our minds, but we can choose whether or not we will entertain them. (or give someone radical permission to choose for us)

What will you do when the old stronghold rears its ugly head?	

✓ Compare your thinking at this point against what 2 Corinthians 10:3-6 tells us to do,

"For though we walk in the flesh, we do not war after the flesh:(For the weapons of our warfare are not carnal, but mighty through God to the pulling down of strongholds;). Casting down imaginations, and every high thing that exalteth itself against the knowledge of God and bringing into captivity every THOUGHT to the obedience of Christ; And having in a readiness to revenge all disobedience, when your obedience is fulfilled."

How are the actions you created tied to changing your thoughts?	

After pondering the previous question, do you need to make any changes to your Action plans? If so, you can go back and adjust.	Go back to your Action Sheet

✓ **Those who get up and spend time in the Word to begin the day are not devoid of problems; they're not devoid of discouragements. They just get over it quicker.**

Disciplines help you follow through and actually do what it takes to accomplish the three actions you created. What disciplines will you put in place to stay on track when the going gets tough?	

What question do you have for yourself?	

Discipline doesn't come without focus, so I want to give you seven bonus points on focus because this so important to your success. I have adapted these specific focus points from The Ohio State University football program, but they apply to life in general.

- Focus is when your mental attention is centered on what you need to do. Nothing else can get into your head
- Focus is when someone can resist temptation in the present to further pursue a goal in the future
- Focus means concentrating on your responsibility.
- Focus means total concentration. Committing to something and staying with it until it is done and done right. Never giving up.
- Focus is the ability to concentrate on something by ignoring outside, important forces that can interfere with the task at hand. Taking advantage of all opportunities that facilitate the task and increase the chances of success.
- Focus is disciplined and zeroed in on the goal and only the goal.
- *"Keep your eyes focused on what is right and look straight ahead to what is good. Be careful what you do, and always do what is right. Don't turn off the road of goodness; keep away from evil paths."* Proverbs 4:25-27

At this point, you have specific and actionable plans for casting down imaginations and bringing your thoughts to the place where you can get your truth back. But you can't go it alone, so next week we identify your Success Partners to **ENHANCE** your plan.

NOTES

Throughout this module, capture your notes, reflections, and ideas in the space below. Feel free to make multiple copies if you need them.

Notes, Reflections, and Ideas

9. ENHANCE IT (Success Partner)

Prepare your Take Back Your Truth Manifesto

Last week you created three actionable strategies. Today, you are ready to wage war with the enemy. Make sure someone has your back. When we go it alone, we are easy prey for the enemy. I want you to find a **SUCCESS PARTNER**. *One who asks how much tangible movement toward your dreams did you make? Rather than simply having someone who holds you accountable, you want a "success" partner who is heavily motivated themselves. A "success" partner is someone to propel you further than you could propel yourself.*

ENHANCE IT - *Proverbs 15:22*

> PRAYER
>
> Father, you know who is best to walk with me through this transformation. If I pick the wrong person, let them say no. I submit to your will not my own. In Jesus' name. Amen.

By adding a Success Partner to your life, you're simply increasing your odds of success. You don't want to lie to someone you respect. So, when you tell them you're going to show up, you're more likely to do so.

Read Ecclesiastics 4:9-12	
What does this mean to you?	

Life is for companionship, not isolation, for intimacy, not loneliness. Prayerfully determine who would be your best success partner.

- ✓ **You should create a network of people who are continually pushing you to live a life pleasing to God and as an example that points to Jesus. Who are your 3 choices?**
    - ☐ _____
    - ☐ _____
    - ☐ _____

✓ **Let's check if your picks meet the criteria. Write the three names across the top column. Test each of the requirements presented. If they don't meet all seven, you should rethink your picks.**

Criteria	1st Person	2nd Person	3rd Person
Someone that is like you, someone with a similar passion and purpose that you want to emulate.			
You understand their strengths and weaknesses. *Set your expectations realistically.*			
This person's morals and ethics align with yours. (They don't have to be in your Church)			
This person takes you seriously and will believe what you are doing is serious.			
This person is trustworthy to keep your conversations confidential.			
Will you asking or meeting bother them? It actually honors them. It shouldn't be a big deal to ask this person to coffee or lunch.			
Can they be a friend? If not, then they're probably not the right Success Partner.			
Do they bring a different perspective than the other 2?			

✓ **Now that you are comfortable with your picks let's prepare to talk to them.**

What perspective do you believe each of the people you listed will bring?	1 2 3

Why are these perspectives essential to your success?	1 2 3

Do you respect them enough to allow them to hold you accountable? *It will happen. You'll get to a point where your Success Partners will feel comfortable enough to call you out. And what you do next is crucial to your growth.*	1 2 3

What will be the hardest part of working with your Success Partners?	

- ✓ **Prepare to tell them your story and your specific ask of them. Concisely accomplish this by creating your *Take Back Your Truth Manifesto.***

    You have to tell them exactly how they can support you.

Your Manifesto will include your Situation, the Complication, and the Resolution.

The mere possession of a vision is not the same as living it, nor can we encourage others with it if we do not, ourselves, understand and follow its truths.

Take Back My Truth Manifesto

This is a Starter Example. Yours should contain much more information.

Situation

o   My stronghold is _____. I realize I am in a war to control my thinking. Thinking that does not align with the Word of God has caused me to _____. I struggle with _____. The root cause of this is _____. It shows up when _____. It has caused me to _____.

Complication

o   The biggest challenge to overcoming it is _____. Unfortunately, it is also affecting _____. I realize they _____. One of the main things I need to stop doing is _____. And one of the main things I need to start doing is _____. This is going to be hard for me because _____.

Resolution

o   To teardown these strongholds and change my thinking, I realize that _____. To get to this place I entered into a process to uncover, unpack, and unlearn the unconscious thinking the enemy had convince me was my truth. This is week 6 of my process and these are the action steps that I will be putting in place to change my thinking and exchange _____ for _____. Action 1 is to _____. Action 2 is _____. Action 3 is to_____. This has been an incredible journey of discovery but I realize I can't do this alone.

I am coming to you because I believe you can add significant value to my process because you _____. I am requesting you be one of my Success Partners. I need you to hold me accountable for _____. I prayerfully selected you when I realized that _____. I have asked _____ and _____ to also be Success Partners because I believe, as the word says, *"a three-fold cord cannot be broken"*. Additionally, they bring _____ to the team.

Would you prayerfully consider walking alongside me through this process?

- ✓ **If you can't clearly articulate this, in writing, go back to step 2 *Explain It* and rework the process. Don't be ashamed if you have to go back; remember the enemy is not going to let go of your mind easily.**

How do you plan to share the Manifesto with them?	

What challenges do you think they will have with your Manifesto?	

How do you plan to overcome that challenge?	

How often will you need to communicate with them? Add that to the Resolution portion of your Manifesto.	

Read Gal 6:1-5	
Do you understand the limits of their support?	

- ✓ **Schedule to meet with them individually for coffee, lunch, or snacks. (Video conferencing is an option if face to face is not an option)**

✓ **Share a copy of your Manifesto and let the conversation flow relationally.**

✓ **Let's evaluate how it went. Answer Yes or No for each question.**

Criteria	1st Person	2nd Person	3rd Person
Did you leave the meeting feeling *better* about yourself?			
Was a connection made?			
Did their thoughts on what the Manifesto says and the direction you are attempting make sense to them?			
Did this person take you seriously and know what you are doing is serious?			
This is not like dating. It's okay to appear overly ambitious. Did they offer additional insights?			

If any question is answered no, feel free to let the relationship go and seek out someone else, instead. You don't have time to waste.

These individuals will be a few of your most critical sources of success. Don't take them lightly, and don't underestimate them. Next week we will begin to **EXECUTE**! Tearing down your old strongholds and getting your truth back.

NOTES

Throughout this module, capture your notes, reflections, and ideas in the space below. Feel free to make multiple copies if you need them.

Notes, Reflections, and Ideas

10. EXECUTE IT (Spiritual Vitality)

Implement your battle plan

Last week you created your Take Back Your Truth Manifesto. Now you're ready to take back the ground you have given up to the enemy. It's time to do battle!!! You have put in the work of unpacking and planning. Now, you have your plan, your Success Partner and most importantly, the Word of God to undergird you.

EXECUTE IT – *Philippians 4:8-9*

> **PRAYER**
>
> Father God, as we go through dark days, we hold on to Romans 8:28, knowing everything is working for our good. Turn crucifixions into resurrections. Be with us in these troubling times. In Jesus' name. Amen

Go back to your three actions and add what the success partners will do to support each action.	
Did you do anything extra or change your original actions after talking with your Success Partners?	
In executing your actions, will you need to involve anyone besides your Success Partners? If so, who? What role will they play in your transformation?	

How do you plan to bring them in the loop? i.e. will you share the Manifesto with them?	

For every stronghold, there's a powerful way to surround it with the truth from God.

- o If you are struggling with a stronghold of depression, surround it with hope.
- o If you are struggling with a stronghold of rejection, surround it with acceptance from the Father.
- o If you are struggling with a stronghold of unresolved anger, surround it with forgiveness.
- o If you are struggling with a stronghold of fear, surround it with the knowledge of God's love.
- o If you are struggling with a stronghold of failure, surround it with the victory of the resurrection.

The mere possession of a vision is not the same as living it, nor can we encourage others with it if we do not, ourselves, understand and follow its truths. To be blessed with vision is not enough . . . we must live them!

✓ **CHARGE!!! Begin executing Action 1**

Resist the sinful patterns of thought that are going to try and distract you.

Remember: this is what you signed up for. Don't wimp out when it gets tough; this is where the really good stuff happens.

What challenges are you experiencing in getting started or in continuing forward with your initiatives?	

Are you effectively utilizing your Success Partners? How? Why or Why not?	

Do you feel controlled by the Spirit that is the abundant life & peace Jesus promised? Why or why not?	

You may be thinking, what will success look like as you go forward? Refer to your Stronghold Worksheets as a measure of your past. And the "How Can You Measure Success" portion of your Action Plans as a measure of the future.

When the enthusiasm for these new actions fade, when the passion cools, when the odds against you increase and the results diminish, when it looks as if success is impossible, will you maintain your intensity and keep going? How?	

We're reaching the end of this journey of discovery, but you will have to keep fighting. The enemy is not going to give up just because you spent the last seven weeks, exposing his lies and deceit. Next week we wrap up this incredible process.

NOTES

Throughout this module, capture your notes, reflections, and ideas in the space below. Feel free to make multiple copies if you need them.

Notes, Reflections, and Ideas

11. ELIMINATE IT (Flourishing)

Teardown your strongholds

You are being made new in the attitude of your MIND. Overcoming your strongholds involved identifying sinful thoughts, comparing them with Biblical truths to stand against evil, finding a Christian support system to walk alongside you, and moving forward by the power of God's Spirit.

ELIMINATE IT

> **PRAYER**
>
> Father God, we thank you for this day. Thank you for reminding us that we must keep our flesh und subjection. Thank you for demonstrating the importance of having a mind that is stayed on you. Keep us safe in your arms. In Jesus name we pray. Amen

After Action 1, move to Action 2. Now move to Action 3 (refer to page 87). You said these three actions would remove your strongholds. We hope this process is blessing you and you are more than a conqueror through Christ Jesus.

What about this process has given you the best insight into your true self?	
Do you feel you have a good grasp on overcoming the stronghold(s) that plagued you?	
Are you progressing?	

Two Rules for Perseverance Rule #1 Take one more step. Rule #2 When you can't take one more step, refer to Rule #1.	Refuse to give up. If you trust God and keep chipping away your change will come.

What do you need to keep doing? What do you need to do differently?	

What has been the most valuable part of this process to you?	

What do you feel was missing from this process that would have helped you even more? Please share this by emailing your answer to me DBYRD@DESTINATIONDESTINY.NET	

Are your Success Partners keeping you motivated?	

12. Euperistatos – The Conclusion

The Greek word *euperistatos*, means well-positioned in every situation. Your carnal sins use to control you because they were well positioned in your mind to ensure their stronghold was secure. By getting your truth back you have transformed your mind, so it is now well positioned to overcome the tricks of the enemy. God has given you weapons with divine power, and you have developed and executed your plan to tear down your stronghold.

> *Wherefore we receiving a kingdom which cannot be moved, let us have grace, whereby we may serve God acceptably with reverence and godly fear: For our God is a consuming fire.*
> *Hebrew 12:28-29*

I leave you with this story:

"During World War II, Lieutenant General Jonathan Mayhew Wainwright was commander of the Allied forces in the Philippines. Following a heroic resistance of enemy forces, he was forced to surrender Corregidor and the survivors of the Philippine campaign to Japan on May 6, 1942.

For three years, he suffered as a prisoner of war in a Manchurian camp. During his internment, he endured the incessant cruelties of malnutrition, physical and verbal abuse, psychological mind games. Through it all, he maintained his dignity as a human being, and as a soldier.

But after the Japanese surrendered the war, his captors kept Wainwright and the other prisoners incarcerated. The war was over, but the bondage continued. One day an Allied plane landed in a field near the prison, and through the fence that surrounded the compound, an airman informed General

Wainwright of the Japanese surrender and the American victory. Yet he and his fellow soldiers were still being kept captive.

Wainwright immediately pulled his emaciated body to attention, turned and marched toward the command house. He burst through the door, marched up to the camp's commanding officer and said, My commander-in-chief has conquered your commander-in-chief. I am now in charge of this camp"[2].

In response to Wainwright's declaration, the officer took off his sword, laid it on the table, and surrendered his command.

God says that our commander-in-chief, Jesus Christ, and our Father has conquered the world and its commander-in-chief who is satan, the devil. What we have is greater than what the world has. And our commander-in-chief has conquered their commander-in-chief, and therefore as General Wainwright said, you need to be in charge of your camp. You are now euperistatos!!!

God doesn't want you to sin. But be confident in knowing that you always have Jesus Christ to give you the strength to overcome so you are *"well-positioned in every situation."*

---

[2] SOURCE: Spiritual Strongholds, Don McMinn, 1993

This is a tool to use going forward. When you're thinking gets off, come back to this tool.

On a scale of 1- 10, please rate the overall effectiveness of this planning process. Please share this by emailing your answer to me <u>dbyrd@destinationdestiny.net</u>	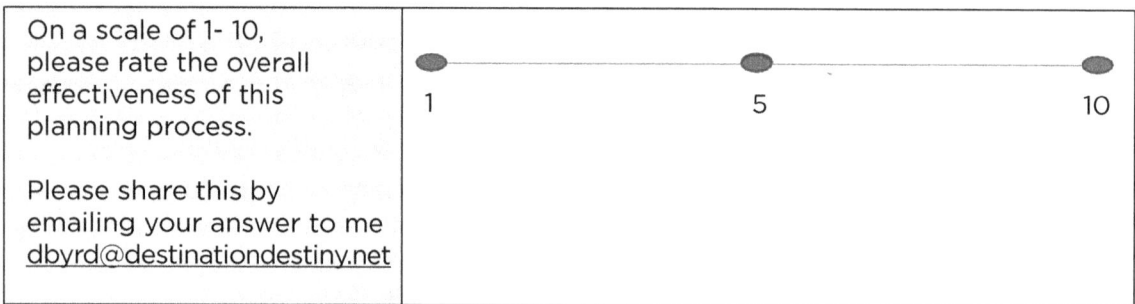

If there is any other way Destination Destiny can serve you, don't hesitate to reach out by phone or email. *Remember, life is a winding road. Choose to keep moving forward, accepting the twist and turns you encounter.*

Stay upon the Wall,

Rev. Dr. I. David Byrd
312.281.1500 | 954.899.0023
<u>dbyrd@destinationdestiny.net</u>

Extra Notes Pages

NOTES

Throughout this module, capture your notes, reflections, and ideas in the space below. Feel free to make multiple copies if you need them.

Notes, Reflections, and Ideas

NOTES

Throughout this module, capture your notes, reflections, and ideas in the space below. Feel free to make multiple copies if you need them.

Notes, Reflections, and Ideas

NOTES

Throughout this module, capture your notes, reflections, and ideas in the space below. Feel free to make multiple copies if you need them.

NOTES

Throughout this module, capture your notes, reflections, and ideas in the space below. Feel free to make multiple copies if you need them.

Notes, Reflections, and Ideas

NOTES

Throughout this module, capture your notes, reflections, and ideas in the space below. Feel free to make multiple copies if you need them.

Notes, Reflections, and Ideas

NOTES

Throughout this module, capture your notes, reflections, and ideas in the space below. Feel free to make multiple copies if you need them.

Notes, Reflections, and Ideas

NOTES

Throughout this module, capture your notes, reflections, and ideas in the space below. Feel free to make multiple copies if you need them.

Notes, Reflections, and Ideas

NOTES

Throughout this module, capture your notes, reflections, and ideas in the space below. Feel free to make multiple copies if you need them.

Notes, Reflections, and Ideas

NOTES

Throughout this module, capture your notes, reflections, and ideas in the space below. Feel free to make multiple copies if you need them.

Notes, Reflections, and Ideas

NOTES

Throughout this module, capture your notes, reflections, and ideas in the space below. Feel free to make multiple copies if you need them.

Notes, Reflections, and Ideas

NOTES

Throughout this module, capture your notes, reflections, and ideas in the space below. Feel free to make multiple copies if you need them.

Notes, Reflections, and Ideas

NOTES

Throughout this module, capture your notes, reflections, and ideas in the space below. Feel free to make multiple copies if you need them.

Notes, Reflections, and Ideas

NOTES

Throughout this module, capture your notes, reflections, and ideas in the space below. Feel free to make multiple copies if you need them.

Notes, Reflections, and Ideas

NOTES

Throughout this module, capture your notes, reflections, and ideas in the space below. Feel free to make multiple copies if you need them.

Notes, Reflections, and Ideas

NOTES

Throughout this module, capture your notes, reflections, and ideas in the space below. Feel free to make multiple copies if you need them.

Notes, Reflections, and Ideas

NOTES

Throughout this module, capture your notes, reflections, and ideas in the space below. Feel free to make multiple copies if you need them.

Notes, Reflections, and Ideas

NOTES

Throughout this module, capture your notes, reflections, and ideas in the space below. Feel free to make multiple copies if you need them.

Notes, Reflections, and Ideas

NOTES

Throughout this module, capture your notes, reflections, and ideas in the space below. Feel free to make multiple copies if you need them.

Notes, Reflections, and Ideas

NOTES

Throughout this module, capture your notes, reflections, and ideas in the space below. Feel free to make multiple copies if you need them.

Notes, Reflections, and Ideas

NOTES

Throughout this module, capture your notes, reflections, and ideas in the space below. Feel free to make multiple copies if you need them.

Notes, Reflections, and Ideas

NOTES

Throughout this module, capture your notes, reflections, and ideas in the space below. Feel free to make multiple copies if you need them.

Notes, Reflections, and Ideas

NOTES

Throughout this module, capture your notes, reflections, and ideas in the space below. Feel free to make multiple copies if you need them.

Notes, Reflections, and Ideas

NOTES

Throughout this module, capture your notes, reflections, and ideas in the space below. Feel free to make multiple copies if you need them.

Notes, Reflections, and Ideas

NOTES

Throughout this module, capture your notes, reflections, and ideas in the space below. Feel free to make multiple copies if you need them.

Notes, Reflections, and Ideas

NOTES

Throughout this module, capture your notes, reflections, and ideas in the space below. Feel free to make multiple copies if you need them.

Notes, Reflections, and Ideas

NOTES

Throughout this module, capture your notes, reflections, and ideas in the space below. Feel free to make multiple copies if you need them.

Notes, Reflections, and Ideas

NOTES

Throughout this module, capture your notes, reflections, and ideas in the space below. Feel free to make multiple copies if you need them.

Notes, Reflections, and Ideas

NOTES

Throughout this module, capture your notes, reflections, and ideas in the space below. Feel free to make multiple copies if you need them.

Notes, Reflections, and Ideas

NOTES

Throughout this module, capture your notes, reflections, and ideas in the space below. Feel free to make multiple copies if you need them.

Notes, Reflections, and Ideas

NOTES

Throughout this module, capture your notes, reflections, and ideas in the space below. Feel free to make multiple copies if you need them.

Notes, Reflections, and Ideas

NOTES

Throughout this module, capture your notes, reflections, and ideas in the space below. Feel free to make multiple copies if you need them.

Notes, Reflections, and Ideas

NOTES

Throughout this module, capture your notes, reflections, and ideas in the space below. Feel free to make multiple copies if you need them.

Notes, Reflections, and Ideas

NOTES

Throughout this module, capture your notes, reflections, and ideas in the space below. Feel free to make multiple copies if you need them.

Notes, Reflections, and Ideas

NOTES

Throughout this module, capture your notes, reflections, and ideas in the space below. Feel free to make multiple copies if you need them.

Notes, Reflections, and Ideas

www.ingramcontent.com/pod-product-compliance
Lightning Source LLC
Chambersburg PA
CBHW050502110426
42742CB00018B/3341